GAMES

If you enjoy reading this book,
you might like to try another story
from the **MAMMOTH READ** series:

NAME GAMES

GAMES

Theresa Breslin

Illustrated by Kay Widdowson

mammoth

First published in Great Britain in 1997 by Mammoth
an imprint of Reed International Books Limited
Michelin House, 81 Fulham Road, London SW3 6RB

Text copyright © 1997 Theresa Breslin
Illustrations copyright © 1997 Kaye Widdowson

The rights of Theresa Breslin and Kaye Widdowson to be
identified as the author and illustrator of this work have
been asserted by them in accordance with the
Copyright, Designs and Patents Act 1988

ISBN 0 7497 2886 8

10 9 8 7 6 5 4 3

A CIP catalogue record for this book is
available from the British Library

Printed in Great Britain by Cox & Wyman Ltd,
Reading, Berkshire

This book is for my friend Jane,
who is never boring

T.B.

One

JANE *HATED* HER name. She didn't just *not* like it. She knew that most people didn't like their names. This was different. Hers she really hated. I mean, *really* hated. As in . . . detest . . . loathe . . . abominate.

She had checked her English thesaurus. There were tons of words that fitted the situation. She had practised saying some of them aloud. If anyone ever asked her what she thought of her name, she would be ready.

'My name,' she would say, 'fills me with a deep and intense sense of disgust.'

It was repulsive and repugnant. It was an

abomination . . . It was also easy to rhyme. And when you had someone in your class like Big-Mac MacLaren, that gave you major problems.

'Jane's a pain,' he would chant as soon as he caught sight of Jane in the playground or cloakroom.

> *'Plain Jane, plain Jane,*
> *She's got no brain,*
> *She is going on a train,*
> *And never will be seen again.'*

'I haven't been on a train for ages,' Jane told her dad one night as she was settling down in bed with her book. She punched her pillow to get comfy. 'It's all your fault,' she said bitterly.

'What is?' asked her dad, flicking through the pages of *The Arabian Nights*, which Jane was reading, trying to find her place for her. He peered at her over the top of his thick glasses. 'Why is it my fault that you haven't been on a train?'

'That's not your fault,' said Jane. 'My *name* is your fault. What made you and Mum choose *Jane*?'

'You are called after your grandmother,' said her dad. 'Jane is a lovely name.'

'No it's not,' said Jane. 'It's completely boring.'

Jane knew this for a fact. Ever since she was small and people had asked, 'What's your name, dear?' she had noticed their eyes glaze over immediately she told them. When she replied 'Jane' they practically yawned in her face. They sometimes tried to make amends by saying quickly, 'That's a good, *sensible* name.'

Whoever wanted a *sensible* name?

Her best friend at that time had been called Giselle. No one had yawned at her. At the playgroup's Christmas pageant Giselle had been chosen to be the Christmas Fairy. It had been the leading role. Jane just *knew* that if she had a more interesting name she would have got that part.

The Name Curse had followed her all the way through infant school and was still with her in primary. Mr McKay, the class teacher, almost never chose her for anything, not even to give out the pencils. It was always someone with an interesting name who was picked, such as Shane who sat beside her, or Juanita and Denzil opposite. Right at this moment the teachers were deciding on the show for the end of term and Jane knew exactly what would happen. No matter what the production was – *Joseph and his Amazing Technicolour Dreamcoat*, *The Sound of Music*, or whatever – she, Jane, would end up being the third reserve scene-shifter.

And then, today, a new girl had arrived. She had stood quietly as Mr McKay had introduced her to the class. Her long, blonde hair, which was softly crimped so that it looked like golden sands just after the tide goes out, hung down to her waist. Her large blue eyes seemed larger and bluer, framed as they were by dark eyebrows and eyelashes. She was tall and stood up straight, gazing out at her new classmates with quiet composure.

I'll bet she's got a terrific name, thought Jane.

She had.

'This is Robertinesca Adellicia Titania Brunelli,' said Mr McKay. 'I want everyone to make her especially welcome.' He picked up his pen. 'My goodness,' he said. 'Your name will take up a whole line in the class register.' He started to write.

Robertinesca Adellicia Titania leaned over his desk. Her long black eyelashes blinked once or twice. 'Adellicia has two l's,' she murmured.

Jane heaved a sigh. Now *that* was a name worth having. A beautiful name, a name to be proud of, a name which commanded respect and admiration. With such an impressive name you could sweep down the staircase at Buckingham Palace, and people would salute or curtsey when you passed by.

Jane sighed again.

Why didn't she have a name like that?

Two

AT SCHOOL THE next day Robertinesca Adellicia Titania was put in Jane's group.

Oh, brilliant, thought Jane as she opened her work book. She looked down at all the cross outs, the blotchy smudges and the spelling mistakes. 'I'll bet Robertinesca never makes any mistakes,' she said to herself.

Jane was right. She didn't.

Jane watched while her new classmate, holding her pencil firmly and confidently, wrote out line after line of perfectly spaced writing.

'Marvellous,' said Mr McKay who had

paused for a moment beside their table to check on progress. 'Well done, Robertinesca! Your writing is an example to us all.'

'I try my best,' replied Robertinesca modestly.

Jane gritted her teeth.

At lunch-time as they waited in line at the serving hatch, Jane heard one of the dinner ladies say, 'That's the new girl, the one with the beautiful name.'

'Oh, yes,' her friend replied. 'It does suit her, doesn't it?'

Robertinesca snatched a plate of food, grabbed a glass of juice, and flung them both on to her tray. Then she marched over to an empty table and crashed the whole lot down on its surface. Two spam fritters bounced off her plate on to the floor.

Jane followed slowly and sat down beside her, 'Umm,' she said. 'Don't you like spam fritters, then?'

Robertinesca Adellicia Titania said a
rude word. A *very* rude word. And then
another.

'Wow!' said Jane, and hoped she'd
remember to check her dictionary when
she got home.

Two large tears crept out of Robertinesca's blue eyes, slid down her nose and
dripped off the end.

Jane hurriedly grabbed a paper tissue and thrust it into her hand. 'What's the matter?'

Robertinesca dabbed daintily at her eyes. 'It's 'cos of what the dinner ladies said,' she sniffed.

'About your name?' A light switched on in Jane's head. 'You don't like it?' she said.

'It is an abomination of a name,' said Robertinesca. She took a deep breath. 'It is repulsive and repugnant,' she paused '. . . and I hate, loathe and detest it.'

Jane gaped at her. She had got *all* the words in, and in only two sentences!

'It's not so bad,' Jane said. 'A bit on the long side perhaps, but . . .'

'A bit on the long side!' shrieked Robertinesca. 'That is an understatement. It takes exactly twenty-three and a half seconds to write it all out properly. Do you realise that most people have finished two and a half pages of an exam before I've even dotted the first i of Adellicia!' She tossed her long hair angrily. 'When I'm older,' she said, 'I'm going to dye my hair purple, cut it short and spiky, wear a biker's jacket and call myself Cath.'

'Yeah, Cath's a good name,' agreed Jane. 'I've often thought of being a Cath. The best bit about that kind of name is that it's *flexible*.' She speared a sausage and chewed the end. 'With a name like that you've got choices, you could be Cathryn . . . or . . . Catharine . . .'

'Cat . . . Cathy . . . Caterina . . . ' Robertinesca went on. She picked up her spam fritters and, wiping them carefully, she put them back on her plate. 'Whereas *I* am stuck with a name that takes up a whole line in the class register.'

'Well it's better than mine,' said Jane. She glanced around her. Big-Mac MacLaren usually appeared at lunch-time, reciting a new rhyme to annoy her with.

'Jane is a completely boring name.'

'At least it's short,' said Robertinesca as she bit into her spam fritter.

'Yeah,' said Jane, 'short and boring.'

At home time there was a little group of mums and dads gathered round a twin pram at the school crossing patrol. Carmen's mum from infant class had brought her new twins – a boy and a girl – out for a walk.

Everyone was oohing and aahing. Jane took a look. The babies were cuddled down together. The boy (in blue) had curly red hair, a flat nose and a determined chin. The girl (in pink) had lots and lots of soft blonde curls and a little rosebud mouth.

'Oh, look at them! Aren't they sweet!' cooed the lollipop lady.

'Yes,' said their mum proudly.

'What cuties!' exclaimed one of the mums, and she tickled the babies under their chins. 'Have you decided on names?'

Jane held her breath.

'Well,' said Carmen's mum, 'we'd thought of Alfie for the boy . . . '

'Oh, yes,' said the lollipop lady at once, 'he looks like an Alfie.'

' . . . and Priscilla for the girl.'

'Absolutely right,' said Juanita's grandpa.

'Perfect,' said Shane's mum.

'Spot on,' said Denzil's dad.

'Awful,' said Jane (but very softly so that no one could hear).

'Jane,' said Carmen's mum, 'would you mind the pram a moment while I button up Carmen's jacket?'

Jane took a firm hold of the handle and gazed with deep sympathy at the two infants. Their bright eyes stared up at her. Deep in their vague blue depths Jane detected the signs of complete panic.

'Help! Help!' they signalled to her.

'Don't look at me,' she said. 'It's not my fault.'

One of them burped and spluttered. The other opened its mouth and then closed it again quickly.

'Too late,' Jane whispered to them. 'It's all been decided for you.'

'Were you dreaming of becoming a male model?' she asked Alfie. 'Then forget it,' she advised him.

'Priscilla,' she told the girl baby quietly, 'if you think you're going to be the first female road construction worker, then you had better get smart, kid. With a name like that they'll stick lace skirts on you as soon as you can toddle. You'll be sent to birthday parties in frilly frocks, pink nail varnish painted on each and every little finger, and wearing tweetie-pie shoes. Your hair will be combed into bunches on each side of your head and tied up with satin ribbons and matching bobbles.

'Alfie,' Jane went on sadly as she shoogled the pram up and down, 'don't try to join the Royal Ballet. Your career path's already set. Digger driver or heavyweight boxer.'

The lollipop lady leaned over and slipped a pound coin into the pram.

'There's a handsel for the new babies,' she said as she put the money under the pillows. 'A little gift for good luck.'

'Good luck!' snorted Jane. 'With names like those, they'll need it.'

These children were cursed. Cursed for life.

Three

J ANE TRAILED HOME gloomily. Champ, the big old tom cat from next door, was stretched out on her garden wall. There were lumps of fur lying on the path and one of his ears had a new looking tear.

'Been fighting again?' Jane asked him when he rose to greet her. She sat down on the wall beside him. 'Given half a chance you probably would have been a pacifist,' she said. 'But it was thrust upon you, wasn't it? Stuck with a name like Champ you now feel obliged to go out and fight with every other animal in the neighbourhood.'

The cat stretched and purred loudly, and then, spotting an unsuspecting sparrow it

made a wild leap into the garden. You would never catch Sintra behaving like that, thought Jane. The sultry Siamese who lived further down the street with the two retired lady school teachers was far too refined to chase birds. Perhaps she longed to . . . maybe she fancied a good roll in the dirt like Champ. But being known as Sintra confined her to a life of surveying the world disdainfully through narrowed turquoise eyes, behind the elegant lace curtains of number thirty-five.

Jane realised that even animals were not exempt.

She went indoors and, dropping her school bag on the kitchen floor, opened the fridge and began to rummage for something to eat.

Her mum glanced up from the evening newspaper. 'Don't spoil your dinner, dear,' she said.

Jane took some juice and sat at the kitchen table. Serena, the little girl from next door, had come to play with Gordon, Jane's young brother. She had brought her collection of Little Dream Donkeys and was carefully brushing their plush grey coats. Gordon was crawling around the floor banging an intergalactic starship into the table legs. The space travellers were flung crazily from side to side when the moon probe landed on the waste bin and then fell into the dog's dish.

Serena's now perfectly groomed donkey family were galloping over the hills of the apples and oranges in the fruit bowl.

Jane watched them for a moment or two.

'Why don't you swop toys?' she asked them.

Gordon shook his head and went on with his game.

'No thank you,' said Serena.

Jane picked up a donkey with long purple eyelashes and a band of flowers on its head.

'Sexist nonsense!' she said crisply. She lifted Gordon's laser blaster and zapped Serena's little donkey into a trillion micro-atoms.

Serena burst into tears.

Jane's mum quickly put down her newspaper and jumped to her feet. 'Whatever's the matter?' she cried. 'For goodness sake, Jane! These two were quite settled until you arrived.'

She glared at Jane as she helped a

24

sobbing Serena to gather up her bits and pieces and then escorted her home.

'I was trying to save her from sexist stereotyping,' Jane explained to her dad later at dinner.

'Well, you can now save to buy her a new donkey,' said Jane's mum. 'That was her favourite.'

'Just because she's called Serena shouldn't mean that she's given traditional female toys to play with,' said Jane. 'We should be trying to break these habits. Parents are responsible for setting boy/girl roles. When I was her age,' she demanded, 'why did you buy me a pram?'

'Because you threw the most amazing temper tantrum in the store until we did,' said her dad helping himself to more potatoes.

'Oh,' said Jane.

'Perhaps you should try not to be so bossy,' suggested her mum. 'You upset Serena terribly, and she is such a sweet child.'

'Yes,' said Jane's dad. 'Try being more composed and mannerly. As Serena is,' he added.

Well that proves my point, thought Jane. Had I been named *Serena* then I would be just that.

Four

IT WAS LIBRARY visit night, and after dinner the family began to round up all their library books. There was the usual delay as they searched for the missing title.

'This happens every week,' complained Jane's dad. 'And may I say, it's never one of *my* books. If you all did as I did and kept your library books in the one place, then they would be much simpler to find.'

This week it was one of Gordon's which had gone A. W. O. L. A He-man and Shera storybook. Jane eventually found it behind dad's bedside cabinet, then they set off in the car.

* * *

'A book of names?' said the librarian.

'Yes,' said Jane, 'I need it fairly urgently.'

'Doing a school project?' asked the librarian as she showed Jane where to look on the shelf.

'No,' said Jane. 'Personal research actually.'

The librarian glanced across to where Jane's mum was sitting with Gordon on her knee, telling him a story. 'Oh . . . oh, I see . . . ' she said.

Jane took a book called *Name that Child* from the shelf. She carried it to a table and opened it up.

There were lists and lists of names. Biblical names, Victorian names, Scottish names, Jewish names, made-up names, Welsh and Irish names. She hadn't realised that there were so many names in the whole wide world. Dozens and dozens and dozens of them. The most popular names since the War, medieval names, the shortest names and the longest ones. Pet names and nicknames. Exquisite names with unusual meanings.

Given that there were so many, and such beautiful and interesting choices, it seemed most unfair that she should be lumbered with *Jane*.

The librarian beamed at Jane's mum as she took her books to be stamped. 'I hope you're keeping well,' she said.

'What?' said Jane's mum. 'Well, yes . . . I am actually. I hope you are too,' she added politely.

'You look after your mum, now,' the librarian instructed Jane as she handed the books over after checking them out. 'Make sure this bag of books is not too heavy for her to carry.'

'Do you think the librarian has been sent on one of those customer care courses?' Jane's mum asked her dad as they drove home in the car.

That night, before she continued reading the tale of *Sinbad the Sailor*, Jane showed her dad the name book from the library.

'Look up my name,' she told him.

He looked.

'Have you found it?' she asked him.

'Uh-uh.'

'Had I been called Jade, whch is directly above, or Jude, which is just below . . . my whole life would have been different,' said Jane.

'Do you think so?' said her dad.

'Yes,' said Jane. 'I mean, how could you do it? You're Jim. Mum's Jean. And you call me Jane. How could you?'

'I told you, you're called after your grandmother,' said her dad. 'That makes it special for us.'

'Well it's not special for me,' said Jane. 'It's incredibly boring. It's so dull no one ever notices me. That's how boring it is.

I'm *never* going to get a part in the school play,' she moaned. 'I don't want to be a Jane any more. I want to be something else. I'd like to change my name.'

Jane's dad took *The Arabian Nights* from her hand and put it to one side. He looked at her very carefully.

'Why don't you then?' he asked.

Jane sat up. 'Can I? Can I really? How?'

'I don't think you have to do anything. Except perhaps fill in an official form called a deed poll. I'll find out for you tomorrow. I suppose you just tell everyone.' He leaned over and kissed her goodnight. 'Remember to let your parents know what you decide, won't you?'

That night Jane had a dream. She was walking in a large garden with many trees and bushes. It was summer and the leaves were green and rustled quietly together. Only, as Jane drew nearer to the trees, she saw that it wasn't leaves which grew there, it was names, each with a different shape, each one separate from the other. And she knew that she was allowed to choose. She could select any one she fancied and it would be hers.

First she took Margaret . . . that name meant 'a pearl'. She was probably of royal descent . . . the Lady Margaret. Courtiers bowed low before her . . .

Now . . . if she picked another leaf . . . She would try Annabel . . . The Annabel she knew was very clever, so from this moment on, she was never going to fail an exam ever again . . .

Jane wandered further in the garden. She reached up to a high branch . . . Let's try . . .

When she awoke the next morning Jane had made a Dramatic Decision.

Five

'SCHEHERAZADE,' SAID JANE firmly.

'Scheherazade?' said Mr McKay.

'Scheherazade,' Jane repeated.

'Why?' said Mr McKay.

'I'm fed up with being a Jane,' she told him, 'and I will be one no longer. I am Scheherazade, the Arabian teller of tales.'

'Oh,' said Mr McKay, 'is that who you are? I think we should stick to Jane for the time being.'

'No,' said Jane. 'Nobody notices Jane. If I stay a Jane person I'm never going to get a part in the school show.'

'Perhaps just in the classroom?'

'No,' said Jane again. 'My dad's seeing about a deed poll. It's my constitutional right.'

'That's true,' said Mr McKay. He opened the class register slowly. 'You're sure about this?' he said.

'Yes,' said Jane.

'Thank goodness your original name didn't take up much room. There's just enough space here for the new one.' He wrote carefully in the register and then showed it to Jane.

Jane looked. He had crossed out Jane's name and written on the line beside it – *Scheherazade Smith*.

Mr McKay put his pen down. 'Jane . . . sorry, Scheherazade, would you like to talk this over?'

Jane shook her head. 'I'm not going to be plain and dull and boring any more,' she said. 'I've changed my name.'

'But being called a certain name doesn't make you a certain type of person,' said Mr McKay.

'I think it does,' said Jane. 'A name is *very* important.'

'Ah, yes,' said Mr McKay softly. ' "What's in a name? That which we call a rose, by any other name would smell as sweet." '

Oh no it wouldn't, Jane thought as she went back to her seat. Try calling it *dog turd*.

'Attention class,' said Mr McKay. 'Jane's name has been changed. From now on she will be known as Scheherazade.'

There was a sudden silence in the classroom. Everyone stared, especially Robertinesca Adellicia Titania.

'I've had a thought,' went on Mr McKay.

The class groaned. When Mr McKay 'had a thought' it usually involved work for them to do.

'We will do a project on names.' He turned and wrote the word on the blackboard. 'Names and their meanings,' he said, 'real or . . . ' he looked at Jane . . . 'imagined.'

The class took their workbooks out.

'Now,' said Mr McKay, 'you will be able to find out lots of information – either in the school or the public library, but I thought we could bounce a few ideas around to start us off.' He sat on the end of his desk. 'Did you know, for instance, that Roman generals used to choose a soldier whose name indicated good fortune to lead their troops into battle.'

'Doesn't sound very fortunate for him,' said Denzil.

'That's true,' laughed Mr McKay.

'Some people are called after jewels,' said Juanita, 'like Ruby or Opal.'

'Or calendar months,' said Niall.

'Yes,' said Mr McKay, 'I'm sure you can think of lots more examples.'

'Animals,' said Big-Mac. 'Leo means lion.'

'And Arnold is an eagle,' said Arnold.

'There are trade names, invented names,

brand names, pop group names,' said Mr McKay. 'Names from all over the world. Did you know that Ayesha became popular because it was the name of the favourite wife of the Prophet Mohammed?'

'Some names sound exactly like the person is,' said Shane. 'Del-boy, for instance.'

'No,' said Mr McKay, 'you're making a link there by association. A successful TV series can set a name to a certain type of character.' He picked up some chalk and went to the blackboard. 'There are words which *do* sound the same as they mean, such as *buzz* or *hiss*. It's known as ONOMATOPOEIA.' He wrote this on the blackboard and underlined it twice. 'And these words can sound the same as they *do*, for example, *bang*. That is also onomatopoeia. But you cannot honestly say that people called Grotty or Grubb, are grotty and grubby.'

Everybody laughed.

'Right,' said Mr McKay. 'Get some headings down. Work in groups. Quietly!' he yelled.

'As they filed out for lunch break Scheherazade Smith gave Big-Mac MacLaren a look of triumph.

'Ha! Big-Mac,' she said to herself. 'Try rhyming that one!'

Six

IN THE DINNER hall Big-Mac
Maclaren came and sat with
Robertinesca and Scheherazade.

'How did you do that?' he asked.

'What?' said Scheherazade (AKA Jane).

'Change your name, like,' said Big-Mac,
and he bit into his burger.

Jane shrugged. 'It's easy. You just register
it, and then there's a bit about a deed poll
or something,' she added vaguely.

'Wish I could do it,' said Big-Mac. He
took another enormous bite of his bun,
and then he stared at it gloomily. 'You
know, I don't really like burgers, but I'm
practically *forced* to eat them every day.'

'But . . . ' said Jane. 'But . . . you do. Everybody knows you do. That's why you're called Big-Mac.'

'No I *don't*,' said Big-Mac. A wistful expression came over his face. 'One of my favourite foods is broccoli quiche, actually. But . . . ' he looked fearfully over his shoulder, 'I'm scared to eat it in public.'

'I don't understand,' said Robertinesca. 'Why does everyone call you Big-Mac?'

'It's all a mistake,' said Big-Mac. 'See, my grandad was really tall, and he always wore a mackintosh. And when I was small I used to call him Big Mac, and then he died when I was still young. I couldn't understand why he never came round to our house any more, so I kept asking for "Big Mac".' Big-Mac heaved a huge sigh. 'My folks just called me Big-Mac as a pet name, and now I'm stuck with it. I come for lunch each day and the dinner ladies say, "Hey, Big-Mac! Here's your Big-Mac!" What can I do?'

He stopped. Bits of onion and beef were sticking out of his mouth, and there was a glob of tomato sauce dribbling down his chin. He wiped them away and put the rest of the burger back on his plate. 'I don't want to eat any more of this,' he said. 'I think now that I actually hate, loathe and detest burgers.'

Scheherazade looked quickly at Robertinesca. She noticed that her new friend's eyes were filling up with tears.

Robertinesca leaned forward and spoke earnestly. 'What *do* you want to do?'

'I want to be a veggie,' said Big-Mac.

'Then why don't you?' said Scheherazade.

'You mean like, now?' said Big-Mac.

'YES!' said Scheherazade and Robertinesca together.

'OK,' said Big-Mac. He stood up. 'Right! From this moment on I'm to be known as Joe.' He squared his shoulders. 'Now I'm going up to the serving hatch to ask for a piece of egg and cress flan.'

In the cloakroom later, the two girls met Pippa.

'I want to get rid of this name,' she said. 'It's given me a complex. Because I was called Pippa I always thought that I should have a brown, curly ponytail and own a horse.' She paused. 'I'm scared of horses. So, I've been to the school library and looked up a good name – Mathilda. It means "Mighty Battlemaid". That's what I'm going to be from now on. "Mighty". Nobody's going to push me around any more.'

Shane was sitting swinging his legs on the end of a bench.

'Our neighbours have a dog called Shane,' he said. 'They give it orders all the time. Our walls are dead thin and you can hear them shouting. "Down!" "Follow!" "Heel!" "Beg!" I think all that noise has leaked through the wall into my mum's brain. That's the way she talks to me now. "Good boy, Shane!" "Sit!" "Go!" "Out!",' he said bitterly. 'I'm getting another name too, even if I only change Shane to Wayne.'

Well, thought Jane, Mr McKay is in for a shock this afternoon.

But when they returned to the class in the afternoon it was Mr McKay who had a surprise for them.

'I've decided to change my name,' he said. 'I want to be called Primrose.'

There were loud guffaws from all around the classroom. But Mr McKay didn't hear them. He was far away to the north, where in the summer, the sun does not set until almost midnight. And he was walking in the dunes on the tiny Hebridean island where he was born. The waves of the

Minch washed against the shore, and the butter-yellow primroses were flowering among the dark green grass. He was a little boy again, and his heart ached for the land he had not seen since he was seven years old. He gave a long, long sigh.

His class stopped laughing.

'Primrose sounds all right to me,' said Joe (AKA Big-Mac). He turned round in his chair and glared at the rest of the class.

'And anyone who disagrees is being sexist,' added Scheherazade.

At that moment the school secretary came into the room with a note. She handed it to Mr Primrose.

'The head has finally decided about the school show,' she said. 'Auditions are at lunch-time tomorrow. Can you let the children know the details, please?'

Mr Primrose took the note and stood up to read it aloud.

'The school's end of term entertainment this year will be . . . ' He stopped and stared at the piece of paper in his hand. Then he swallowed hard and began again. 'This year our school will perform the musical show called . . . *Calamity Jane*.'

Seven

'*CALAMITY JANE!*' Scheherazade repeated the name her teacher had just read out. She turned to Robertinesca and scowled. 'Unreal,' she said.

As soon as she got a chance Scheherazade went over to where the class dictionary was kept on the window-sill. She checked the meaning of the word calamity. 'Serious misfortune,' it said. 'A disaster.'

Too right, she thought.

There was only one thing for it. She would have to change her name back again before the auditions.

'You can't do that,' Robertinesca told her. 'Everyone knows you're Scheherazade now. And anyway,' she looked around quickly, and then lowered her voice, 'people might think you were only doing it to get the best part in the play.'

'As if!' said Jane scornfully.

The next day a large group of would-be actors and actresses gathered in the assembly hall at lunch-time. Ms Elgin, the drama instructor, explained that *Calamity Jane* was a musical, and the story took place in a town in the American Wild West. There would be lots of stamping and clapping and singing. The main character was a girl called Jane who was a really lively person. Then Ms Elgin divided them into two groups for male and female part readings. She wrote down all the boys' names on her clipboard and then began to take the girls'.

'Name please?' she asked the girl at the top of the queue.

'Jane,' came the reply.

'That's handy,' smiled Ms Elgin. 'And you?'

'Jane,' said the girl who was standing behind the first.

Ms Elgin wrote them both down. 'Next,' she said.

'Jane,' said the third girl in line.

'Well, this should make it easy for who-ever's typing the cast list,' said Ms Elgin. She looked at the fourth girl, who stared straight back at her and said . . . 'Jane.'

What a coincidence!' said Ms Elgin. 'Who is next?'

'Jane,' declared number five.

'Really?' asked Ms Elgin.

'Yes.' Leigh-Ann McArthur nodded her head vigorously.

Ms Elgin hesitated and then went on.

'Jane,' asserted girl six.

'Ms Elgin wrote the name down very slowly. She looked nervously at the following girl in the line.

'Jane,' Su Lin Cheng said firmly.

Ms Elgin didn't say anything. She only raised her eyebrows as the next girl came forward.

'Jane,' declared Dominique Bennett.

'Oh dear,' said Ms Elgin faintly.

At Jane Number Nine she finally stopped writing.

'Ummm . . . ' she said, pencil hovering

over her clipboard. She thought for a moment. 'I wonder,' she paused, 'I wonder . . . would it be simpler if I just gave everybody a number?' she asked. 'And then, I'll call them out in order, shall I?' She tucked her pencil behind her ear. 'Otherwise we are all going to get terribly confused. Especially me,' she added under her breath.

Maybe Mr Primrose was right, thought Scheherazade as she walked home from school later that afternoon. Perhaps being called a certain name didn't make you a particular kind of person. She took her script and costume notes out of her jacket pocket and studied them. She would make a very good cowgirl she thought. So, there were eleven other cowgirls, but who cared? At least she hadn't behaved in the pathetic manner of those girls in the assembly hall at lunch-time. Imagine! Changing your name in order to get a part in the school show. How sad!

She read Ms Elgin's costume suggestions. Hat, necktie, checked shirt, fancy waistcoat, boots. She would have a good rummage in her dad's wardrobe. She was sure that there was a leather waistcoat there that he had hardly ever worn. With some fringes sewn on, it would be perfect.

'We Stagecoach Girls are sittin' on top
of the world
Yellin' out loud, and givin' our lassoes
a twirl
Here we come! Step out of the way!
Zippity doooda! Zippity daaay!'

Scheherazade sang loudly, inaccurately and out of tune, as she turned in at her gate.

She gave a few practised stamps of her cowboy boots on the garden path before opening the front door.

Eight

THE NEXT DAY, in school, Mr Primrose announced to his class that he was going to stop being a Primrose, and remain a McKay for the time being. He had signed the wrong name when buying petrol that morning and the garage attendant had kept his credit card and called the police.

Then Shane said that his mum was really upset last night when he told her he was changing his name. She had called him Shane after her favourite film star, and now that he was Wayne instead of Shane it just wouldn't be the same. She had promised in future she wouldn't shout,

'Here, Boy!' or bang a spoon on a plate when his dinner was ready. So he had agreed to become Shane again.

Doris told Mr McKay that her dad had said she *must* change her name back to Anastasia. If she didn't go back to being Anastasia, then her great aunt, after whom she had been named, said she was cutting her dad out of her will *immediately*. She certainly wasn't going to leave her money to someone with a child called *Doris*. Though Doris's (now returned to being Anastasia's) mum had said she didn't mind. Everyone knew the silly old bat hadn't any money anyway. Someone who believed that they had once been the Grand Duchess of all the Russias must be completely off their rocker.

'How interesting,' said Mr McKay when Anastasia told him all of this. He stopped with his pen in the air. 'Any other changes?'

Nobody spoke.

'I'll keep the register open,' said Mr McKay, 'just in case.'

At first break there was a huge row.

Denzil had a fight in the playground with Deepankar in Room Six. Denzil had swopped his name with Deepankar yesterday, and now wanted it back. Deepankar (as was), now Denzil, said no way, he wasn't giving it back. It was his. It had been a fair swop, properly agreed, witnesses present, and he was keeping his new name.

Then Mathilda, who had been Pippa, thought that she now preferred Balzinder. But there was a girl in Room Nine already called Balzinder and, up until then, she had been the only person in the whole school with that name. She wasn't happy that someone was copying her.

Lots and lots of pupils, boys and girls, had decided that Jackie was 'their very favouritest' name. There were now twenty-three Jackies in one class.

At lunch-time, Mr McKay made an announcement.

'Far be it for me to interfere with anyone's civic rights,' he said, 'but these are exceptional circumstances. In the interests of World Peace I must ask that everyone now revert to their original names. In any case, it would appear that you cannot individually record a deed poll until you are eighteen.'

Jane was secretly glad. Scheherazade was *extremely* difficult to spell. And, she hadn't appreciated quite how *comfortable* a name Jane was.

There was also the matter of the school show . . .

Ms Elgin had commented, as she wrote down Jane's new name, that fitting 'Scheherazade' on to the poster for the show might be rather difficult.

Mr McKay reached again for his bottle

of Tipp-Ex. 'Perhaps,' he said, as he began to rewrite the register, 'we might consider that it is not the *name* that is you.' He looked around at his class. 'Perhaps you just have to be yourself, so that people appreciate *you* first and then learn your name.'

'Well,' said Big-Mac MacLaren, 'I've decided I *want* to be known as Big-Mac. It reminds me of my grandad. But I'm still going to eat nut loaf and cheese and onion pasties,' he added.

'What made you choose Joe?' Jane asked him. 'Did you think that was the name a veggie would have?'

'No,' said Big-Mac. 'It's my real name actually.'

Robertinesca gave a great sigh. 'My parents won't allow me to shorten or abbreviate my name,' she said. 'What am I going to do? Eighteen is a long time away.'

'We could just use your initials,' said Big-Mac. He spelled them out.

'R-A-T.' He grabbed the end of Robertinesca's long hair and gave it a quick tug. 'How about being called Ratty?' he asked.

Robertinesca Adellicia Titania gave Big-

Mac a huge grin. 'Thank you,' she said.
'Thank you so much. You have set me free.'

Big-Mac's face went red. 'Don't
mention it,' he said.

That night, as Jane was falling asleep,
she had a sudden thought. She didn't have
to stick absolutely to Jane, did she? She
could alter it a little, without changing it
completely . . .

She could be *Janette* . . .

Janine . . .

even *Jasmine* . . . ?